I0756011

FINISHING LINE PRESS
www.finishinglinepress.com

THE BOXWOOD MAZE

poems by

JIM SMITH

Finishing Line Press
Georgetown, Kentucky

THE BOXWOOD MAZE

Copyright © 2026 by Jim Smith
ISBN 979-8-89990-358-8 First Edition
All rights reserved under International and Pan-American Copyright Conventions. No part of this book may be reproduced in any manner whatsoever without written permission from the publisher, except in the case of brief quotations embodied in critical articles and reviews.

Publisher: Leah Huete de Maines
Editor: Christen Kincaid
Cover Art: *The Unfortunate Lover*, circa 1530
Author Painting: Phyllis Mayes
Cover Design: Elizabeth Maines McCleavy

Order online: www.finishinglinepress.com
also available on amazon.com

Author inquiries and mail orders:
Finishing Line Press
PO Box 1626
Georgetown, Kentucky 40324
USA

Contents

The pennycandystore beyond the El
is where I first fell in love
with unreality

—Ferlinghetti

INNOCENCE

The Boxwood Maze

Stay where you are. Don't move
an inch. Sitting on a bench
in the boxwood maze.
Wearing the yellow dress
you wore to church Sunday morning
when I asked you to go out walking.

I still have the photograph,
probably in a book somewhere.
You in the afternoon light,
the sun at my back,
my shadow reaching out to you.
Your 18-year-old smile
promising every sin in the Catechism.

Perhaps we'll walk hand in hand
through the labyrinth. Into dark secret places.
Hansel and Gretel forgetting to leave a trail.
Theseus and Ariadne searching for a monster.
Laughing when we reach a dead end,
lost in each other.

Around a corner, the monster.
You'll go one way. I'll go another.
Sometimes running into each other.
One of us always running away.
Stay where you are. Sitting on that bench,
the sun at my back,
my shadow never reaching you.

Self Portrait as a Don Martin Cartoon

After years of work with his psychiatrist, Mister Fonebone
walks down the street, carefully repeating his mantra:
I do not look like a plate of spaghetti and meatballs!

The premise is Mad Magazine nuts, cooked and exaggerated.
No one would really think he looked like an Italian dinner—
pasta dreadlocks and meatballs where the eyeballs should be.

I could never eat spaghetti without red sauce staining my shirt.
And those meatballs! I had no idea what was in there—
some small docile animal ground up and rolled into a ball.

In the cartoon conclusion, a plate of spaghetti and meatballs
lands on Mister Fonebone's head—and he doesn't even notice,
still repeating the incantation: *I do not look like a plate of…*

My character was confirmed and confused by Don Martin.
I learned to walk down the street in complete confidence
while checking my reflection in storefront windows.

The Well

You Asked For It was the best
TV show in the whole wide world.
Sunday night at 7:00 you could see
suspension bridges twisting in the wind

till they snapped, gigantic machines
tunneling into the earth, men wrestling
big snakes—all sponsored by Skippy.
But my 9-year-old little Sister's

favorite TV show was *Lassie*—
Sentimental dripping claptrap
about an adorable boy and his dog
acting in a fake television barnyard

every Sunday night at 7:00.
It didn't matter what I wanted to watch,
Sister would always get her way.
She yelled the loudest. She was a girl.

I ran outside in bright red anger—
I could not be in the same room as Lassie
or hear that stupid whistling theme song
that drove me absolutely crazy.

Sunday night: Smash! Crash! Arf!
Lassie stormed into the living room!
"What is it?" said Sister, "Tell me!
Did Timmy fall down the well?"

The Campbell's Soup commercial ended.
Sister applauded as *Lassie* came on.
Television actors acted worried
when little Timmy didn't come home.

It's been quite a while waiting down here,
our TV shows have long been canceled.
Occasionally I glimpse a star passing by
or the face of a dog, concerned.

The Great Debate, 1960

Mother took us kids to see Kennedy,
the first Catholic running for President,
who didn't have a snowball's chance.
But first
we went to St. Joseph's on the Brandywine,
where we all took communion
even my mean little sister.

Father took me to the Republican Rally
to cheer Nixon on his waltz to the White House.
But first
we went duck hunting, up before dawn,
slogged through a slough by the Brandywine.
He shot at a bird that dropped from the sky,
but it still had some life
so Father broke its neck.

Kennedy's airplane descended from the clouds,
his daughter's name on the fuselage.
So many people were singing,
"He's got high apple pie in the sky hopes."
He said
American citizens are starving in Appalachia,
the poverty rate is appalling,
unbefitting a nation aspiring to greatness.
Later my sister jumped the fence
and Kennedy shook her hand.

Nixon jumped right up on the stage,
everyone in Chester County was there.
His jokes didn't make sense to me
but the crowd was laughing anyway.
He said
The only reason Americans go to bed hungry
is they're too God-damned lazy
to get off the couch and go to the refrigerator.
Driving home, Father said, "Wasn't that great?"
and I thought of that poor dead duck.

At Longwood

George Nash lived across the yard,
our lawns separated by a row of bushes,
which I accidentally mostly mowed down
when I was too young to drive the big mower
that Dad borrowed from his job at Longwood.

His daughter—what was her name?
Pattie? On hot midsummer nights
she played piano with her window open
and annoyingly kept me awake
after I was forced to go to bed at 7:30
even though it was still light out.

Dad would get on Mr. Nash about his hair
which he never seemed to cut comb or wash.
Proud of his stint in the US Army, Dad
always got his hair cut close as possible
with the #1 hair clippers (#2 was for me).

But at Longwood, George Nash
was in charge of the Rose House
and the DuPonts with their chauffeured Rolls
and the Mennonite girls giggling in bare feet
swooned at the sight and scent
of ceaseless roses perfectly pruned.

The Problem with Genes

If Mary hadn't joined the chorus of the Brandywiners at Longwood Gardens
even though she was a lousy singer
and met Smitty who had been working as a gardener ever since he dropped
out of school after the seventh grade
and if he hadn't offered her a ride home
and if Mary's father hadn't gotten over his doubts about the four Smith boys
who had a reputation for drinking and wrecking cars
although Mary said her man was the best of the lot
and if they hadn't married on a January day in the sacristy of Saint Patrick's
instead of the nave because he was a Presbyterian
and if right before the vows she hadn't won their first argument
by making him take his warm coat off
and if after the war they hadn't had a daughter Elizabeth
who inherited the gene for singing from her father
who later in life sang in a barbershop quartet
and if Elizabeth hadn't seen My Fair Lady in a touring production
and decided to audition for the Brandywiners
where she was discovered by a 42-year-old music teacher
who thought she was wonderful and wanted to find her a job singing
at a resort in the Poconos although she was only 16
and if her parents hadn't said absolutely not
then Elizabeth could have been a Broadway star instead of marrying
a shopkeeper and giving birth to two boys
who between them could not sing a note.

You Good Dog You

My dog ran off with a total stranger, happily climbed
in his pickup truck, with nary a glance behind.
I threw her clothes on the sidewalk—
that little green number I found at Saks,
the blue sailor suit—Aww, she looked so cute.

Fluffy and Spike ran rough down the Coast,
knocked off six or 7-11s, outsmarted the guard at PetSmart,
always making a clean getaway
like Warren Beatty and Faye Dunaway,
her head out the window brazenly barking.

Holed up in some flea-bag motel, a ratfink cat
ratted them out. Police surrounded them screaming,
Come out! Keep your paws in the air!

Worthless old Spike he copped a plea—The bitch set me up.
The judge he agreed, sent Fluff up the river
for 14 years—to her more like 98.

She shared a cell with a sadistic Shih Tzu,
pumped iron in the prison yard,
sharpened her teeth like a buzz saw,
till the night of the howling moon
Fluffy managed to chew her way through the bars.

The prodigal pooch pawed at my door, badly needing a bath
and shampoo, preferably one with a fresh citrus scent.
I took her in, because that's what I do.
I told her to stay, and that's what she did.

Signs and Wonders

Under the rug in my sister's bedroom
was a lump about the size and shape
of a rat. It remained a mystery for ages
and we were both too scared to take a look.
Whatever it was, we figured it must be dead,
but I teased her, saying, Oh no that's not true,
the sneaky creature's only biding its time
and one night it will crawl into your bed
then eat you alive while you're sleeping.

So we passed though childhood and we grew
into serious adults. I saw her less and less.
She called me before work one morning.
I could hardly hear her whisper the news
that she had found a lump in her breast.

What I Did Last Night

I was not flying
though surfing that giant wave out of the woods was loads of fun
and I nearly got to ride in a dogsled but first the grass had to be mowed.

I was not late for class
though I overslept two hours while Susan kept waiting
and I wish I had tied my sneakers in time to play ball with Michael Jordan.

I did not see any monsters
though I had to fight off a million flies trying to get in my car
and the moon suddenly sinking below the horizon was a little bit scary.

I did not notice any Freudian parts
though Patty never gave me a kiss like that
and a train going by with the passengers waving must have meant something.

My family and friends dropped by,
including the lady from poetry class who had painted her house
and my father drove a golf cart guiding me safely through dangerous hedges.

Make no mistake, they were out to get me.
They dumped a truckload of garbage in front of my house
and when I jumped on the hood of that car they tried to arrest me.

It was like clicking through TV channels
catching snippets of a hundred boring movies
and although I'm a terrible actor I was there in every scene.

Two Stories, Once Removed

Mother loved to tell this story: While living
on Willow Street, having just turned 17,
blooming like a riot of apple blossoms,
she waited for this curly-haired dreamboat,
name of Bill Walsh, to take her motoring.
She wore a fashionably draped 1933 outfit
and told her doting father she wouldn't be late,
not too late. He cast a parental look, said,
"You're not going anywhere dressed up like that."
When the doorbell rang, she was mortified
as her father took an Irish linen handkerchief
and pushed it down between her breasts to hide
that exposed and lonesome valley near her heart.

And now the story's mine: When mother lay dying
on Linden Street, losing her senses at 71,
like the fading flowers on a Christmas cactus,
she was determined not to receive visitors
afraid she looked too awful in her condition.
The doorbell rang, I greeted an elderly man
with gray curly hair, and asked mother if she
would see Mr. Walsh. She sighed, replied,
"But all the past has drained away, it's late,
it's much too late." His head sagged, "Oh well,
tell her I expressed my everlasting concern.
I mostly came by because I wanted to return
a crumpled-up Irish linen handkerchief."

Oranges and Snails

in the Protestant Cemetery, Rome

Behind the small Egyptian pyramid
among neat rows of dark green boxwoods
an orange tree has burst into bloom
announcing the turn of another spring.
The fruit drops against the tombstones
but no weeping angel stirs his marble wings
no distinguished head blinks his bronze eyes
no sad cherub breaks into a heavenly smile
no bella signora climbs down off her bier
and no poet complains about his epitaph.

In time the oranges split open, spilling
their sour nectar, attracting the snails
that move imperceptibly, slow as another century,
across a stone: *Sacred to the memory of Anne Bythia*
who died at Rome on the 2.d April 1844 aged 61 years
As mistress, friend, sister, daughter, mother, and wife,
her conduct through life was most exemplary
and she never caused pain but by her death.

The Fairies

Geppetto wanted a boy but the wooden puppet he made
fell flat on its face. The Blue Fairy said, *Tell you what,*
I'll give free will to that Woodenhead, and if he proves
to be brave and unselfish, I'll turn him into flesh and blood.
After Pinocchio made several bad decisions, hung out
with the wrong crowd, and got swallowed by a whale,
the Fairy said, *Okay Geppetto, there's your boy.*

Elsie and Frances had been playing in the garden
with their friends the Fairies and took some photographs,
causing a sensation at the Theosophical Society
which considered them evidence of a better world.
Then came the depression and a war and the people
forgot about Fairies, who only wanted to flutter about,
alight on flowers, and sip the morning dew.

Every evening as the sun sets on the via Labicana,
completely deserted on account of the invisible plague,
Moira leans out of her window and takes a photograph
showing the Green Fairy looking for children to play with.
But the children are forbidden to go outside because,
it is said, that unless they prove to be brave and unselfish,
the Fairy will change them into wooden puppets.

Virginia Slim

In an old sepia newsreel,
grandpa catches grandma
hiding in the laundry room
sneaking a nasty smoke.
Cut to today's woman,
bopping down the street,
in her hand a cigarette,
swinging fine and free.
Slim as a fashion model,
cool as a breath of air,
she flashes a radiant smile,
does what she wants to do.
So smart, so very modern,
she's a self-reliant lady,
you've come a long way.

First the yellow cough,
but it's not her fault,
caught in cruel addiction,
still there's always hope.
They cut the rot away,
they couldn't cut it all;
the doctor says he's sorry,
the pendulum swings back.
Slim as a starving child,
she breathes a little sigh,
buys time with radiation,
there's nothing else to do.
No pain, no medication,
she's quiet and polite,
she's only here a while.

Here After

I wouldn't let those memories get to me
cleaning out her last place of residence

Not the radio that hadn't worked since 1955
or the TV that only got public television

Nor the shoebox full of photographs
of smiling brides and unknown relatives

Not her jewelry bold enough for a queen
or knickknack notions of very good dogs

Nor a copy of Anne and her Green Gables
or a book full of scary fairy tales

Not the chair from which she navigated
the narrow passage of her final days

Nor winter coats bound for the thrift store
minus her favorite still keeping her warm

Not her slippers or expensive shoes
the ones that I wanted her to wear

But I broke at seeing the empty dresses,
colorful ghosts ready to dance till dawn

Breaking Up

The bonfire out, I went looking for the one who brought me—
a 1961 Chevy, pearly white, automatic with power steering.
She and I hung around together, though she wasn't my type.

George and I headed home, trying to stay between the lines—
promptly got lost—having lived here all our lives. I said
"George, where are we?" he said "I'm not George, I'm Tuggle".

Joe Tuggle had his name tattooed on his knuckles—did it himself—
but he left off the little hook on the "J" so it read "Toe".
His family lived next to Strodes, they made really good scrapple.

Rounding the curve on Rt 52, I said "Here we go George!"
Into the trees! I was on the ground laughing my fool head off.
Tuggle cut the ignition—that car tried to run me over.

So the Chevy and I finally broke up, and I started dating
a 1965 Mustang, dark green, four on the floor, 200 horsepower.
And George still says he remembers being in the accident.

A Locked Room

No obvious signs of a struggle—
windows shut tight, no broken glass,
the room securely locked from inside.
A half-eaten breakfast, coffee still hot,

windows shut tight, no broken glass.
At first glance nothing seems amiss—
a half-eaten breakfast, coffee still hot,
the knife remains in the kitchen drawer.

At first glance nothing seems amiss.
I'll get to the bottom of this.
The knife remains in the kitchen drawer.
Didn't I have the means and motive?

I'll get to the bottom of this.
Where was I on the night before?
Didn't I have the means and motive?
My footprints across the floor.

Where was I on the night before?
The room securely locked from inside,
my footprints across the floor,
no obvious signs of a struggle.

Theories of Evolution

Antarctic winter in total darkness,
thermometer down to minus forty,
I sledged through snow
for five excruciating weeks
to collect emperor penguin eggs
whose embryo development
might prove or disprove the theory
that birds evolved from reptiles.

My niece carried her unborn child
through the New Hampshire winter,
which brought snow every day,
for forty grueling weeks
and gave birth to a human boy
whom she named Axle
to prove or disprove the theory
that boys evolve into motorcycles.

ADVENTURE

Broadway Bound

In my other life I carried a switchblade,
lived in a rundown West Side tenement,
my greasy hair combed in a cool DA.
Strutting down the alley, this delinquent
would start a rumble, then plead I'm innocent
when nabbed by kindly Sergeant Krupke.

To my chagrin, Sister had all the talent—
as she frequently reminded me,
I lacked any trace of musical ability.
But while Betsy banged on the piano,
we sang together a joyous cacophony
of sharps and flats and traumatized notes:
We're disturbed! We're psychologic'ly disturbed!
The next door neighbors no doubt concurred.

Police Check Theatre in Hunt for Convict

At 2:45 pm an unidentified woman called Police Headquarters, saying that she was "entering the Roxy Theatre with a criminal recently escaped from the borough prison". Policemen from four precincts converged on the crowded theatre where they found 6,000 people enjoying a comedy act, a juggler, real live lions, and a gaggle of geese. The flatfoots worked their way down the aisles, carefully scrutinizing the patrons. As if we all aren't criminals, brought into this world with original sin—thanks to Adam and especially Eve—set up for crimes of commission or, for the timid, those of omission.

The Mayor sought to head off this crime wave, imagining punks growing up on the West Side snapping their fingers, dancing wildly, brandishing switchblades. He ordered the police to find all male children under two years of age and mercilessly put the sword to them. But it was only a wild goose chase. At 6:30 pm a call to the Roxy Theatre declared "there was no use in the police staying around because they were no longer there". The clever woman and her newborn son had fled into Egypt.

One From the Heart

The angina was only an annoying pain
dedicated to the odds of writing well.
The anxiety led to fibrillation
as my precious junkpile of words
disjointed started to collapse.

Calliope dropped by, and informed me, in verse,
she knew a bit about cardiovascular surgery
and desperately, urgently, I needed to be edited.
So she performed a sternotomy,
split my breastbone with her ballpoint pen.

She spoke, in perfect metrical speech:
"Let's crank up the oxygenator,
you've been breathing dusty everyday language.
Look at those lines of alleged verse,
they're as hard as arteriosclerosis.
Your carotid arteries are clogged
with a lifeless buildup of tongue-tied phrases
and over-inflated metaphors.
And those aneurysms in the chamber walls
indicate a scurvy of fresh ideas."

The mitral valve couldn't keep her out.
The aortic valve didn't even try.
Calliope moved right in, stapled my sternum shut,
sewed up the old pericardium
and gave me a ream of blank paper.

Mt. Holyoke in the Sixties

We were allowed to knit in class
though it wasn't a requirement.
That click clack metronome
helped me get an education—
with every row a lesson learned.
Somehow it didn't drive the teacher crazy.

The girl next to me in Classical Studies
said she was knitting a sweater for her lover
but couldn't decide which one.
To myself I thought,
whether she knew it or not,
she was making a shroud.

Then on the last day of class—
right in front of our teacher—
she slowly carefully pulled on the thread
until that beautiful sweater
and everything she had learned
unraveled.

Villanova in the Sixties

We weren't allowed to smoke in class
but the air in the stairway was toxic.
Had to wear a jacket and tie
to every class, to every meal—
after all, it was a Catholic school.

Freshman year I employed the old Windsor Knot—
balanced symmetrical conforming.
By senior year I adopted a simple overhand knot
cocked to one side. I had firm opinions,
read too much, thought I was smart.
Got interested in poetry,
heard about the mess in Southeast Asia.
I wore the ugliest combination of shirt and tie.
I was a rebel.

Like that kid next to me in Theology class
whose hair was long and might have had a mustache.
Who wore jeans that were holy and frayed
(along with a jacket and tie).
Who on the last day of class,
as some sort of protest, I guess,
pulled out a cigarette lighter and set fire to his pants
but he quickly snuffed it out
unlike some monk on a street in Saigon.

Belle of the Ghazanelle

She's in the garden wearing gossamer lace;
her shadow crosses the sun in total eclipse.

I'm trying to remember that fabulous face
somewhere under a curtain of Belgium lace.

She no longer plays the sweet little miss;
prominences rage behind her black eclipse.

Still I'm convinced she's substantially chaste
despite the trail of trampled Queen Anne's lace.

I believe she promised me one tender kiss
if I ever escape this suffocating eclipse.

After all she's held together by spit and paste
and the thin swiss cheese of Chantilly lace.

The sun reappears from her devious eclipse;
wickedly laughing she parts the curtain of lace.

Eating the Sun

At the Alburgh VT eclipse festival, children sit at a picnic table drawing the sun with black crayons. A dragonfly brushes my cheek. It's time I checked the astronomical charts. At breakfast a man curses hell. My grandfather's dying, he promised to wait. It's a ten-hour drive. A friendly snake circles my ankle. Sorry, I'm only passing through. Even the air smells like maple syrup. On the playground the kids swing so high they might hit their heads on the moon. Grandfather feels a chill, needs a coat. The darkness crawling once again as in those pesky nightmares. Unfazed by fireworks, the dragon snaps. I take one last look around. In Vermont, the children stay up late playing hide and seek in the dark.

This Page Intentionally Blank

Flip the switch that disconnects the machinery of your senses till the mind goes blank and the lake appears under summer skies while you glide your canoe celebrating the silence with no sea shanty sailors or talkative guides then you find a mirror cove the clouds seem to drift underneath as the slish of swirling water curlicues off your paddle like the curl of a girl underwater floating in flowing medieval gown with a blank stare singing how should I your true love know now you want to embrace her stay in the scene till you see a specter approaching nearer neither submarine nor welcome party for he is the keeper of possibility whose thwack of his tail sends you retreating to town where you search for revelations on a blank wall.

Treatise on Nature Poems

Nature needs no poetry
Keep your simple similes to yourself
A babbling brook's got plenty to say, not to you

Birds on a wire sing for each other
An alligator won't work as an allegory
A lamb is not a sweet iamb

The fog doesn't come in on little feet
Exploding volcanoes form massive caesuras
The ocean is deeper than any see

Clouds look down you're just an allusion
The sun sports a crown it's best not to look
The wind blows forward the wind blows back

Sunsets aren't sad and mornings aren't melodious
The moon and stars don't belong in a couplet
You can't know what happens after dark

An octopus does fine without an ink pen
Nature is writing thousand-page novels
Rain will erase your 26-character trash

The woods aren't lovely or lonely
Leaves fall dead, come back in the spring
But if truth be told, you won't

Washing the Wall

Night passed without incident
as white-haired men moved in
wearing remnants of old uniforms,
bearing buckets, sponges, brushes.

The names were honored by bugles,
the names chiseled in granite,
sharp as a military salute,
sharp as jagged shrapnel.

The men scrubbed and scraped.
The men rubbed and cursed,
applied a ton of elbow grease,
strained their poor old backs.

Soap and water flew everywhere,
removed the caked red mud,
removed the traces of blood,
until the cleaning was done.

Dawn streamed over the ages.
Marble gleamed in the light,
reflected their worn-out faces,
dejected, disappointed, sad.

Despite all their efforts,
despite all their foolish notions,
not one single name
not one single name was erased.

Fade to Black

A cloud or some dragon swallows the sun,
the hole in the sky encircles your brain.
Quick in the house, upstairs to the bedroom,
close your door careful no one can hear;
someone is watching, pull down the shades,
think like a burglar, extinguish the lights.

Spider webs spin themselves around you,
footprints trail off in the carbon dust,
going to be here near a thousand years.
Hurry, dive under the blanket, the quilt
your mother sewed together, each panel
remembering a disappointment or pain.

Inside should be safe, don't make any
sudden movements. The floor drops out,
down the well you fall, past the roots,
the reasons not buried quite deep enough.
Now get hold of yourself for a second,
try to describe the subtle shades of color.

PFC Marchand

Take one step forward!
nobody moved
Get out of here, you're all in the Army!
Tom was like me, college graduate, from a nearby town,
now prisoners on the train to perdition.
We stopped in DC for a few hours.
If any of you get off this train you'll be court martialed!
Tom's friends took him out for a night of carousing.

At Fort Bragg we got one hour off Sunday morning.
Tom went to Mass.
When he returned he was laughing like hell.
said he had a long discussion with a statue of Jesus.
His friends had given him a tab of LSD.
After that, Tom seemed to buy into the nonsense,
he did the best he could.
I even caught him spit-shining his boots.

We both shipped out to Vietnam,
assigned to different infantry divisions.
I made it back home
and read about Tom in the local newspaper.
With complete disregard for his own personal safety,
Pfc. Marchand continued evacuating his comrades.
While he was returning with the last wounded man,
the enemy unleashed an intense line of fire.

Two Years Later

In the first days of my destiny,
during a downpour, illuminated by lightning,
sheltered by a cheap plastic tarpaulin,
I lay beside the redhead Anna Salamone,
pretending to be a hippie
(to the dismay of my father).
We were encouraged "do your thing"
and freaks did a snake dance across the hill,
crazed by fiddles, guitars, and banjos,
in a farmer's field at the '67 Folk Festival.

In a rice paddy within the Iron Triangle,
armed with rifles, grenades, and claymores,
we watched for the enemy across the hill,
doing what we were ordered to do
(silently cursing our fathers).
We pretended to be soldiers,
me and my closest friend Jim Szczur,
huddled under a camouflaged blanket
during a downpour, unnerved by lightning,
in the last days of my delusion.

War Souvenir

I spent a week with the rat patrol
checking the road for booby traps.
Larry talked about his girl in Georgia;
he carried a picture of Lisa smiling
beneath the magnolias,
wearing a pure white dress.

We passed through a country
where we didn't belong,
sent to preserve somebody's freedom.

Soldiers believe there's no greater bond
than the one between brothers in arms.

Larry told me he killed a man,
not for hate nor for glory.
His squad was ambushed one night—
Larry kept shooting into the dark,
into the heart of a stranger.

Buddhists believe we are bound
to an endless cycle of birth and rebirth.

Next morning he didn't rejoice
when he found the twisted corpse
of the man who tried to destroy him.

Larry shouldn't have taken his wallet;
he showed me the picture inside—
a girlfriend or wife reaching out
to touch a lotus flower,
wearing a pure white dress.

Life Story

It was only a place to be born
one as good as another
Eighteen years of goofing off
earned the rank of citizen
A letter from the elders
services must be rendered

It was only a camp in the woods
a little like being in boy scouts
A really bad haircut
too much off the top
A free suit of clothes
one color one size fits all

It was only a walk through the wire
with backpack and bandolier
A sunny day in the country
tropical plants closed their eyes
Sunburned out of water
a couple of blisters bleeding

It was only a bit of straw
left behind in the field
A momentary lapse of attention
daydreaming words to a song
A single step forward
never heard the concussion

It was only a place to leave behind
one as good as another

Veterans' Banquet

While the red white and ragged flag stumbled down the floor
old men in leather vests covered by exclamations lamentations
sucked in their guts silently saluted,

while the American Legion left them for dead they swore almighty
never again will one generation of veterans abandon another
until the last man breathing,

while selling t-shirts advertising PTSD the disabled complained
lousy compensation Democrats denied what heroes deserved
Agent Orange to blame for mortality,

while those who took bullets in stride swallowed rockets red lead
stood before the television crew shed a tear trembled remembered
their homecoming somebody spit,

while corn-fed Christians sold $3,000 tickets to see the miracle
heal the wounds play championship golf believe it the war is over
Viet Cong love democracy love all of us,

while wives threw fits about seating arrangements when sitting
next to strangers eating chicken with their grubby hands
who refused to pass the rolls,

while the after dinner Marine said damn good job jar-headed maggots
you should be proud 3,000,000 enemy dead wins the prize
freedom preserved like peaches,

while the best of a brave generation managed to stand on their feet
cheering ovation hooray not a single one noticed
I lay upon the floor still bleeding.

Where One Does Not Belong

Papa-San walks to work across an open field
A carnival cardboard duck pulled by a string
        Step right up—Ten cents a shot
The soldiers think he cannot be trusted
probably a spy or at least a sympathizer
        They fire a couple mortar rounds at him
When the smoke and noise subside
        Papa-San stands up and walks away

After the war, a veteran drives to North Philly
looking to score a quarter ounce
        His coat and tie out of place in the Badlands
The drug runners consider this moving target
        Win a prize—Ten cents a shot
The veteran slowly cruises down the street
A cardboard duck being pulled by a string
        wrapped tightly around his neck

Reading the Names

Reading aloud to the dead
Taking your place in line
A million words unsaid

Soldiers outside of time
Reading the names in the dark
Taking your place in line

An open wound to the heart
A high school photo remains
Reading the names in the dark

But the narrative stays the same
A leaden night without a moon
A high school photo remains

Where flowers refuse to bloom
The name of your best friend
A leaden night without a moon

The name of your brother
Reading aloud to the dead
The name of your father
A million words unsaid

Return to the Scene

I lost my Saint Christopher right around here.
There's no point in looking for it now,
everything's been plowed under—
the huts built from empty ammunition boxes,
the showers that were seldom used,
the helicopter pad, the hospital tent.

I wrote to her about the constant heat,
the peasant lady who gave me rice cookies,
the old man walking home from his field,
those spectacular tropical sunsets.

I told her I read "The Armies of the Night"
—did they really levitate The Pentagon?
My days were spent playing double solitaire,
filling sandbags as if a storm was coming,
listening to Lennon sing "Don't Let Me Down".

I didn't think she wanted all the truth—
the monkeys, the spiders, the leeches, the rats.
Or my nights outside the concertina wire
walking very, very carefully,
lugging a radio, collapsible shovel,
enough firepower to overthrow a small country,
and a 4 x 7 inch field dressing bandage.

Why didn't she write me back? Even a little note
"Be safe" would have been nice. Oh well.
My luck disappeared with Saint Christopher,
but everything's back to normal,
the past has been plowed under.

ROMANCE

Poetry, Interrupted

There's a man on the railroad tracks
head down reciting his verse—
something about adversity, futility.
He rails on and on,
one of those interminable pieces.

A westbound freight
is a comin' round the bend,
chugging trochee trochee trochee...
The whistle shatters the air
in horrid—hooting stanza—

The obstinate fool keeps reading.
You'd think he would know
you can't stop a train with just a quatrain.

The freight cars chase each other's tails,
full of compressed gas, worthless scrap.
And out the locomotive window,
the engineer is waving
the latest copy of *Passager*.

The poor man's verse was pretty
bad, but this is worse.
The cars rumble by, a tragedy unfolding
in dactyls—clickety clackity...
leaving behind a cloud
of self-addressed stamped envelopes.

But the poet rises from the dirt
and continues reading his elegy
to the crumpled corpse of poetry.

Time Was When

The moon she moves imperceptibly,
the eye cannot distinguish. Evolution
ignores the subtle in favor of the sudden—
like falling rocks and poisoned arrows.

If I balance the moon upon a branch,
or sight along the curve of Claire's leg
while she lies in the grass delectably,
and hold my head so very still, I think
I see the change. Was it me that moved?
The shadow on my retina isn't there.

Nature sends her memos faithfully—
the first crocus on a cold March morning,
a withered garden in the last of August.
Was it once in bloom? I never noticed
the yellow creep along the vine. I didn't
see it coming, this arrow in my heart.

Arthur's Wedding Day

Here we are, at the perfect place—
the Royal Observatory, Greenwich—
zero hour at zero longitude.
The suspended sun hangs at its apex
on the longest day of the year.
We're waiting for the orb to drop,
one more tick of the clock, Guinevere,
until our hemispheres meld together.
I'm so nervous I can't recall this morning,
or for that matter, how I courted you
or even the day we met.

Here we are, at the Prime Meridian,
with friends of the bride on the west,
knights and dusty pages on the east.
Merlin remembers the future
but has no knowledge of the past.
He says we honeymooned in a castle,
lived like kings never needing a thing,
until you met your Lancelot.
But that lies far ahead, or is it far behind?

Here we are, at the pinnacle of our lives,
still waiting for time to fall from the sky.
I'm anxious to see how we'll meet,
maybe a glance in a small café,
maybe I'll pull a sword from a stone.

Ode to Anna Nicole

How you stunned us at first sight
crossing the horizon, big as the sky
more blonde than the summer sun.
A triumph of engineering—
air-brushed torpedo, hydrogen dream
above the prairies of America.
Adolescent boys, passions stirred
by the prow of the new Hindenburg.

As you drifted over Texas
longhorns and decrepit billionaires
offered you their hearts
as if that could ever be enough.
You passed over the Capitol
tourists pointed to the sky
at our new national monument.
The Supreme Court voted
nine to nothing, unanimous—
you're the most glamorous.

Now you're flying into Lakehurst,
a summer storm is threatening.
Lightning strikes, hydrogen ignites
your glory explodes in flames
falling, falling, nothing but bones.
Grown men weep, such a calamity,
a grievous loss to humanity.
Farewell, farewell, Anna Nicole—
you were greater than any hyperbole.

At Breakfast

When I play Cowboys and Indians seems I always get shot or tomahawked no difference if I'm a good guy or not. The blonde in the pink satin nightgown keeps bothering me with girly giggling while I grind the mountain-grown beans. I tell her about my cowboy dream camping by the fire singing a lonesome song me and my horse beside our selves. I stir my coffee with a dapple of cream hiding from the cops as a pixie-haircutted girl whispers they'll never find us here. The police searching high searching low I sip my coffee. With Cheerio good cheer she asks would I like her to conjure some Chocolate Frosted Sugar Bombs with a dollop of milk. I pull out my guitar let me sing you a cowboy song with hardly hidden glee she says this time I'll be the bad guy points a finger bang you're dead and I say no I'm not.

Brideshead Revisited

The heart is not a paper valentine
presented to that boy in the library
Like the Writer studying at Oxford
finds he doesn't know the rules
of play at the teddy bear picnic
Or the Catholic Girl thinking
she found herself a decent man
too married to be her husband.

The heart is not a jigsaw puzzle
assembled in leisurely evenings
Like two Orphans of the Storm
strolling together on the rolling deck
alone somewhere in the ocean
Two lovesick Orphans thinking
the pieces of their broken hearts
fit so perfectly together.

The heart is carved from Italian marble
heavy as Roman antiquities
Like the Catholic Girl learns her heart
had been cemented inside a wall
of the church when she was baptized
Or the Writer soaked with salt water
who drops his heart which rolls away
and sinks somewhere in the ocean.

Grass

Catherine's mother warned her, Keep off the grass,
there's rusty nails and worse: the poisonous
snakes that hiss come hither, you parochial
girls who lollygag yourselves home after Mass.

The devil himself understands what lurks
beyond the concrete edge of earth; the slimy
serpents gone to wrap themselves about your shiny
pedal pushers. Even the slightest smudge of dirt
could leave your soft white soul in bad condition;
the venial sins that spread like some disease,
a black consuming plague of mortal danger.

Catherine heard her mother's admonition,
she stayed on the sidewalk, always right on track
until that awful day she stepped on a crack.

The Office of Religious Affairs

Religion is a locked-room mystery.
My gift was a mistake, I admit.
She suffered for her blasphemy.

On the desk, it kept her company—
a small totem pole made by the Inuit.
Religion is a locked-room mystery.

My friend read the sacred litany.
I never considered her a heretic
who could suffer for her blasphemy.

The wooden eagle wings led to tragedy,
for the college was Roman Catholic.
Religion is a locked-room mystery.

The Dean soon arrived at an epiphany—
that pagan cross was not a crucifix.
She suffered for her blasphemy.

Now Religious Affairs has a vacancy.
My cautionary tale is terrible, isn't it?
Religion is a locked-room mystery.
There is suffering in blasphemy.

A Gentleman Calls

He said he'll arrive right after dark, there's so much to do.
I bought a choice cut of steak. That's what men seem to like.
He's bringing the wine, Burgundy with an old, old vintage.
We'll need some music, Dean Martin's on the turntable.

Take my hair out of curlers. God, I look so pale.
Add gobs of makeup, enough to look natural.
What to wear, what to wear? Ah, that dress with the lace collar.
Hey, it finally fits, I guess I've lost some weight.
Where did I put my necklace? The one with the lucky charm.

On the phone he sounded distinguished, probably sports a beard.
Bragged about his accomplishments—lord of this, lord of that.
I believe him, but I don't believe him.
I wonder how he got this number?

I'm giddy as a schoolgirl. Always did my lessons.
What to talk about? Something highfalutin, like Milton or Dante?
Wish I could get rid of this cough.
At last, someone took an interest in me.
Always thought of myself as plain, a plain little life.

Everyone said be patient, my prince will come.
Been waiting like Sleeping Beauty under glass.
Might as well use the good china. If not now, when?
Baked a chocolate cake for dessert—dark, very dark

Paean to a Poem

The camera glides over the snow
toward a fairytale ice-covered dacha.
In the darkened parlor Yuri Zhivago
fumbles to light a candle—
the red dawn offers no hope of heat.
With frozen fingers he begins to write
his famous love poem to Lara.

Yuri burned with interior intensity—
I hardly noticed he wrote in English.
Each line perfect, no revision required.
In the midst of revolution and slaughter
(nicely filmed in widescreen Panavision),
in the middle of a 3-hour spectacle,
I heard the heart of poetry.

Count me out of any revolution.
I'm not cut out for marching—
prefer putting words down on paper.
I could write a love poem
if only I had a mustache like Omar Sharif,
if only Julie Christie, longing and joyful,
was waiting for me upstairs.

Frozen

Natasha in the spring said she's leaving;
for no reason I keep on believing.

I'm headed out to drown in vodka
when I know I should be bereaving.

Her heart's as cold as Stalingrad;
it's futile to continue besieging.

This lamb is meek, my mood is mild;
this little heart is bleating.

I used to take her breath away
(she pretended she wasn't breathing).

Red is the color of revolution.
Scarlet my hopes are bleeding.

She said it wasn't the mud or crud
just her new wings a-beating.

Natasha was constant as Lenin's Tomb;
I still can't believe she's leaving.

The Ice Hotel

The bar a slab of ice, the souvenir glasses ice
from an applejack martini. Our wedding reception
thudded a dud the polar bears weren't nearly as amusing
as I had hoped. Ice. Ice took down the Titanic
the prettiest girls fled fast to the lifeboats
their beaus bid a fare-thee-well fair sex.
Arctic ice she knows no mercy.

What a perfect place for our honeymoon, $600 a night
might well be worth it. Did you notice those sculptures?
Venus popping out of a half shell shivering
while a Minotaur is dragging some gal away
too skimpily dressed for northern climes.
Nothing Arctic ever melts.

Our room comes with an ice xylophone I don't
have a musical bone but if one of us gets bored
I'll play you a happy tune. The fireplace is carved
from ice the logs of course they're ice a light
flickering like fire. I wasn't fooled for a second.
No fire can melt Arctic ice.

The bed solid ice we're under the skins of caribou, musk ox,
beaver, and fox, those who died for us. Beside me
you're reading Doctor Zhivago, he's almost frozen
ice on his mustache while his fingers scratch
a poem to Lara. Your feet are cold, your breath the smoke
of a wolf howling on the side of a mountain.
Your Arctic heart will never melt.

Splendidly Smashed

Past closing time at the Pink Pachyderm,
Mr. Lindsay Anderson of East Belfast
set out to smash
the Guinness world record for crawling a mile,
possessed
like Livingston seeking the source of the Nile.

After downing one final Guinness Stout,
to his mates' wild shouts,
he wobbled down the cobblestone street
on hands and knees,
a toddler who had just learned to crawl
obsessed
with catching up to a glittering ball.

Onward he pressed, he would not rest, until
Success!
In a record 23 minutes and 44 seconds,
he reached his home address
where Mrs. Anderson,
in hair curlers and pink night dress,
said she was not impressed.

An Elephant Walks Into the Room

When I squeezed through the door
no one said a word. I know who
did what. Who's running off
with whom, or wishes they had the nerve.
Who drinks bourbon from the bottom.
No priest will offer them penance.
May be a play where the drama
lies under the silence; a word
can split a cozy narrative. I'm leaving
undaunted. I'll saunter myself
back to the jungle, take their petty
angst away. I'm big enough to hold
all the secrets of the world,
which I promptly forget.

Forget Me Not

What did you say your name was?
Would you like to hear me sing?
My mind's as sharp as it never was.
It's my birthday, what did you bring?

Would you like to hear me sing?
I forgot I can't carry a tune.
It's my birthday, what did you bring?
I should be getting out of here soon.

I forgot I can't carry a tune,
Being kept under heavy sedation.
I should be getting out of here soon,
Searching for better accommodations.

Being kept under heavy sedation,
Everyone appears to be disappearing,
Searching for better accommodations.
Don't shout, I'm not hard of hearing.

Everyone appears to be disappearing.
My mind's as sharp as it never was.
Don't shout, I'm not hard of hearing.
What did you say your name was?

Wending Down

In class I learned
the value of matches.
The fire started in a seam

underneath our town,
turned it into a wasteland.
To me that seemed poetic.

Everyone moved away
but you, you said you saw
a sparkle in my eye

though I smelled a little
like smoke. Oh no, said I,
isn't it Ash Wednesday?

Dust to dust,
just like Mr. Eliot?
She called me a blooming idiot.

Our opposites ignited,
we stopped dropped and rolled
onto the bearskin rug

before the roaring fireplace,
which gave a lovely light.
I said it looks like creation.

She told me I know nothing,
her candle burns at both ends,
this could be our night.

We snuggled in cozy
flames till nothing remained,
from the kindling in my head

to my pocket full of posey.
Ashes, ashes,
we all fall down.

Nursery Rhyme

Please file calmly out the door.
There'll be no death-defying here.
I only commiserate with the mouse,
give him dinner. He offers spiritual advice.
We ponder the inexplicable:
why the dish ran away with the spoon
till midnight chimes like chocolate,
my heart still going tickety tock
as the mouse and I run up the clock.

ACKNOWLEDGMENTS

Grateful acknowledgment is made to the editors of the following publications in which these poems first appeared.

Gargoyle: “Mount Holyoak in the Sixties”, “Villanova in the Sixties”

Mid-Atlantic Review: “Eating the Sun”, “This Page Intentionally Blank”

0-Dark-Thirty: “Two Years Later”, “War Souvenir”

One Hundred Poems for Hearing Dogs: “You Good Dog You”

Passager: “The Great Debate, 1960”, “Poetry, Interrupted”, “Return to the Scene”

Poems Against War: “Washing the Wall”

The Quarterday Review: ‘Splendidly Smashed”, “Frozen (Ghazal)”

Whirlwind: “Veterans’ Banquet”

Wordland: “Fade to Black” (Earlier version)

Jim (James Ernest) Smith grew up with flowers and fountains in idyllic Longwood Gardens PA, matriculated at Villanova University in the 1960s, discovered Ferlinghetti and the Beat Poets, and began to write poetry. He was told by a teacher that his verse was technically okay but he needed more experiences in the real world. After graduation, Jim was immediately drafted and sent to the rice paddies of Vietnam as a grunt; he lived through it, and wrote about it. His next 40 years were spent with the US Bureau of Labor Statistics, first in Philadelphia and then in Washington DC, all the while continuing to write.

After retirement in 2011, Jim honed his craft through classes at the Writers Center in Bethesda MD and workshops with outstanding poets. His readings have enlivened local book stores, libraries, and the Kensington Book Festival. On Memorial Day and Veterans Day, he has joined readers at the Vietnam Veterans Memorial.

Active in veterans' causes, Jim works with incarcerated veterans during visits to Maryland State Prisons. Also, he is regularly beaten at golf by his sister Maryann. To this day, Jim honors the memory of Baa, the best dog in the world.

Jim's pieces have appeared in terrific journals such as *Passager, Gargoyle,* and the *Mid-Atlantic Review*. In 2024, he received honorable mention from *Mid-Atlantic* for the Luce Prize, which is awarded to emerging poets.

The Boxwood Maze is his first published poetry collection. Jim lives in Silver Spring MD with his wife the wonderful artist Phyllis Mayes.

www.ingramcontent.com/pod-product-compliance
Lightning Source LLC
LaVergne TN
LVHW090536110826
845146LV00003B/1127

* 9 7 9 8 8 9 9 9 0 3 5 8 8 *